SUPER SPIDERS
WOLF SPIDERS

BY LISA J. AMSTUTZ

PEBBLE
a capstone imprint

Published by Pebble, an imprint of Capstone
1710 Roe Crest Drive, North Mankato, Minnesota 56003
www.capstonepub.com

Copyright © 2026 by Capstone. All rights reserved. No part of this publication may be reproduced in whole or in part, or stored in a retrieval system, or transmitted in any form or by any means, electronic, mechanical, photocopying, recording, or otherwise, without written permission of the publisher.

Library of Congress Cataloging-in-Publication Data is available on the Library of Congress website.
ISBN: 9798875224973 (hardcover)
ISBN: 9798875224546 (paperback)
ISBN: 9798875224935 (ebook PDF)

Summary: An introduction to wolf spiders, including where they live, what their bodies look like, how they hunt their prey, and more.

Editorial Credits
Editor: Ashley Kuehl; Designer: Bobbie Nuytten; Media Researcher: Svetlana Zhurkin; Production Specialist: Whitney Schaefer

Image Credits
Alamy: Nick Upton, 17; Capstone: Kay Fraser (grass and spiderweb), cover and throughout; Getty Images: Anton Petrus, 5, 8; Newscom: imageBROKER/Emanuele Biggi, 19, Photoshot/NHPA/Anthony Bannister, 14; Shutterstock: All Write studio (spiderweb), 4, 10, 14, Cathy Keifer, 13, 15, 18, Danut Vieru (spider), cover, back cover, 1, John Navajo, 10, kerim danatarov, 6, Lukas Jonaitis, 9, Macronatura, 7, 16, Petr Malyshev, 20 (middle), Shane Rooney 89, 20 (bottom), Steven Ellingson, 11, Vida Shams, 4

Any additional websites and resources referenced in this book are not maintained, authorized, or sponsored by Capstone. All product and company names are trademarks™ or registered® trademarks of their respective holders.

TABLE OF CONTENTS

All About Wolf Spiders 4

On the Hunt.. 10

The Cycle of Life 14

Spider Hunt 20

Spider Jokes 21

Glossary 22

Read More 23

Internet Sites 23

Index 24

About the Author 24

Words in **bold** are in the glossary.

ALL ABOUT WOLF SPIDERS

A big, hairy animal **stalks** its **prey**. It bares its big **fangs**. *Leap! Chomp!* The creature catches its meal.

What is this hungry hunter? A wolf? No! It is a wolf spider. But it hunts like a wolf. That is where it gets its name.

Wolf spiders live in many parts of the world. You can find them in rainforests and deserts. Some live in grasslands. Others live on mountains. You might even find one in your basement!

Wolf spiders live alone. Some dig **burrows** to live in. They may line them with **silk**. There, they can hide from **predators**. Others just roam. They hide under rocks or logs.

Wolf spiders can be brown or black. They often have stripes on their back. These spiders can be as small as a grain of rice. Or they can be as big as your hand!

Wolf spiders have eight eyes. There are four small ones in a row. There are two big ones above them. Above that are two more.

ON THE HUNT

A wolf spider uses its many eyes to hunt. It does not make a web to catch food. It sits and watches for prey. Wolf spiders eat bugs and other spiders. They can even eat small frogs or snakes.

Here comes a bug! The spider dashes after it. It grabs the bug with its strong legs. *Slice!* The spider's sharp fangs sink in. **Venom** flows into the bug. It soon dies. Its insides turn to mush. The spider sips them up. Its mouth is like a straw.

THE CYCLE OF LIFE

It is time to find a **mate**. A male waves his long **palps** or drums them on a leaf. He finds a female to mate with.

The female lays eggs in a silk sac. She sticks it to her back end. It looks like she is dragging a big ball. She keeps her eggs safe from predators.

It is time for the eggs to hatch. The female bites the sac. *Pop!* Tiny spiders spill out. They climb on their mother's back. She carries them for a week or so.

Each baby feeds on its yolk sac. Then the babies leave. They will find homes of their own.

The wolf spider is the world's most common spider. You may have seen one. They are fun to watch. It is best not to touch them, though. Wolf spiders can bite! Their bite will not make you sick. But it can hurt!

SPIDER HUNT

Did you know that you can spot wolf spiders at night? Use a flashlight to search outside after dark.

What You Do:

1. Go out to an open grassy area on a dark night.

2. Hold a flashlight at your eye level.

3. Sweep the beam over the ground.

4. Look for glowing green eyes 15 to 20 feet (4.6 to 6 meters) ahead. Those are wolf spiders!

SPIDER JOKES

What do you get when you cross a spider with a snowman?

frostbite

What kind of spider comes out under a full moon?

A wolf spider!

Why did the fly fly?

Because the spider spied her.

What do you call it when you have too many spiders in your backyard?

a no-fly zone

GLOSSARY

burrow (BUR-oh)—a hole in the ground made or used by an animal

fang (FANG)—the biting part of a spider's mouth

mate (MATE)—to join together to produce young

palps (PALPS)—a large pair of mouthparts

predator (PRED-uh-tur)—an animal that hunts other animals for food

prey (PRAY)—an animal hunted by another animal for food

silk (SILK)—long, thin threads made by a spider

stalk (STAWK)—to hunt an animal in a quiet, sneaky way

venom (VEN-uhm)—a poisonous liquid produced by some animals

READ MORE

Becker, Becca. *Wolf Spiders*. Minneapolis: Jump!, Inc., 2025.

Humphrey, Natalie. *Wolf Spider vs. Tiger*. New York: Gareth Stevens Publishing, 2023.

Pettiford, Rebecca. *Spiders*. Minneapolis: Bellwether Media, 2025.

INTERNET SITES

Australian Museum: Wolf Spiders
australian.museum/learn/animals/spiders/wolf-spiders/

BioKIDS: Kids' Inquiry of Diverse Species—Lycosidae
biokids.umich.edu/critters/Lycosidae/

Britannica Kids: Spider
kids.britannica.com/kids/article/spider/353800

INDEX

babies, 16, 17
biting, 16, 18
burrows, 7

eggs, 15, 16
eyes, 9, 10

fangs, 4, 12
food, 4, 10, 12, 17

hunting, 5, 10

mating, 14

venom, 12

webs, 10

ABOUT THE AUTHOR

Lisa Amstutz is the author of more than 150 children's books on topics ranging from applesauce to zebra mussels. An ecologist by training, she enjoys sharing her love of nature with kids. Lisa lives on a small farm with her family.